Fa

3D

Else Plantinga

FORTE PUBLISHERS

Contents

© 2004 Forte Uitgevers, Utrecht
© 2004 for the translation by the publisher
Original title: *Fairyland in 3D*

All rights reserved.
No part of this publication may be copied, stored in an electronic file or made public, in any form or in any way whatsoever, either electronically, mechanically, by photocopying or any other form of recording, without the publisher's prior written permission.

ISBN 90 5877 459 7

This is a publication from
Forte Publishers BV
P.O. Box 1394
3500 BJ Utrecht
The Netherlands

For more information about the creative books available from Forte Uitgevers:
www.forteuitgevers.nl

Final editing: Gina Kors-Lambers, Steenwijk, the Netherlands
Photography and digital image editing: Fotografie Gerhard Witteveen, Apeldoorn, the Netherlands
Cover and inner design:
BADE creatieve communicatie, Baarn, the Netherlands
Translation: Michael Ford, TextCase, Hilversum, the Netherlands

Preface	3
Techniques	4
Materials	5
Fairyland	6
Dancing elves	10
Elves on a tree-stump	14
In love	16
Elf on a toadstool	19
Swan elves	22
Fairy-tale wedding	26
Christmas in Fairyland	30

Preface

When I think of Fairyland, I see a dream world with elves and fantasy figures. The pictures which I have used are so pretty that they do not need anything extra. You do not even have to add glitter, because this has already been printed on them. If you do not want to make the cards 3D, then you can also only use one picture, because they are really attractive just by themselves. Some cards have been made with embroidery and others have been made using embossing templates.

Whilst making these cards, I sometimes imagined myself in a fairy-tale world. I hope that you will as well.

Else

I would like to thank Anja Timmerman for making this book possible and my partner, Egbert, who did everything possible to ensure that these wonderful pictures were made available to everybody.

Techniques

3D cutting
To make 3D pictures, you need 3, 4 or sometimes 5 pictures which are the same. The Fairyland cutting sheets which are used in this book have 18 to 20 pictures on them which are the same. Cutting patterns of all the cutting sheets used are given in this book. They show how many pictures you need to use and in which order they must be stuck on the card. Cut out the first picture and stick it on the card. Next, cut out the other parts and carefully shape them using a 3D shaping tool. Apply 3D glue to the back of the cut out pieces, turn them over and carefully stick them on the first picture. It is easier and makes less mess if you use a pair of tweezers to do this.

Embossing
Place an embossing template on the part of the card that you wish to emboss and stick it in place using non-permanent adhesive tape. Turn the template and the card over and place them on a light box. Use an embossing stylus to lightly press the lines of the embossing template to create a relief pattern in the paper.

Cutting and embroidery
I have used embroidery templates and cutting templates in this book. Place the cutting template or the embroidery template on the card and stick it in place using non-permanent adhesive tape. Cut out the shapes or prick the holes of the embroidery template. Look at the photographs in this book to see how the card must be cut or what the embroidery must look like.

Punching
Some cards have an unusual punch pattern. This is made by using two Paper Shapers. Use punch 1 first and then punch 2.

no. 1   *no. 2*

Materials

- Card: De Hobbyzolder (H) and Papicolor (P)
- Fairyland cutting sheets: Else Pantinga Design
- Embossing templates
- Light box
- Embossing stylus
- Embroidery templates
- Sulky metallic embroidery thread
- Sticker sheets
- Hobby pens
- Adhesive stones
- Design knife
- Cutting mat
- Perforating tool
- Pricking mat
- 3D shaping tool
- 3D glue

Fairyland

1. Cat with half a star

What you need
- Card: brilliant silver (P162) and metallic (P143)
- Sticker sheet: silver borders
- Hobby pen: green
- Embossing template: EF18024
- Sulky thread: metallic mint
- Adhesive stones
- Fairyland cutting sheet: Cat (GW01)
- Stickles

Make a card which measures 15 x 21 cm. Place the template on the front of the card and stick it in place. Draw the shapes that you wish to cut out and prick the holes in the template. Do the embroidery before cutting out the shapes. Stick green card behind the openings. Cut out the picture and stick it on the card. Cut out the separate parts according to the pattern, shape them and stick them on the background picture. Colour the border sticker green and stick it between the embroidery. Use glitter to make a couple of dots.

2. Cat with half stars in a curve

What you need
- Card: brilliant silver (P162) and metallic (P143)
- Sticker sheet: silver borders
- Hobby pen: green
- Embossing template: EF18024
- Sulky thread: metallic mint
- Adhesive stones
- Fairyland cutting sheet: Cat (GW01)

Make a card which measures 13 x 26 cm. Use a pencil to draw quarter of a circle on the card (see diagram 1) so that you know where to place the

FAIRYLAND

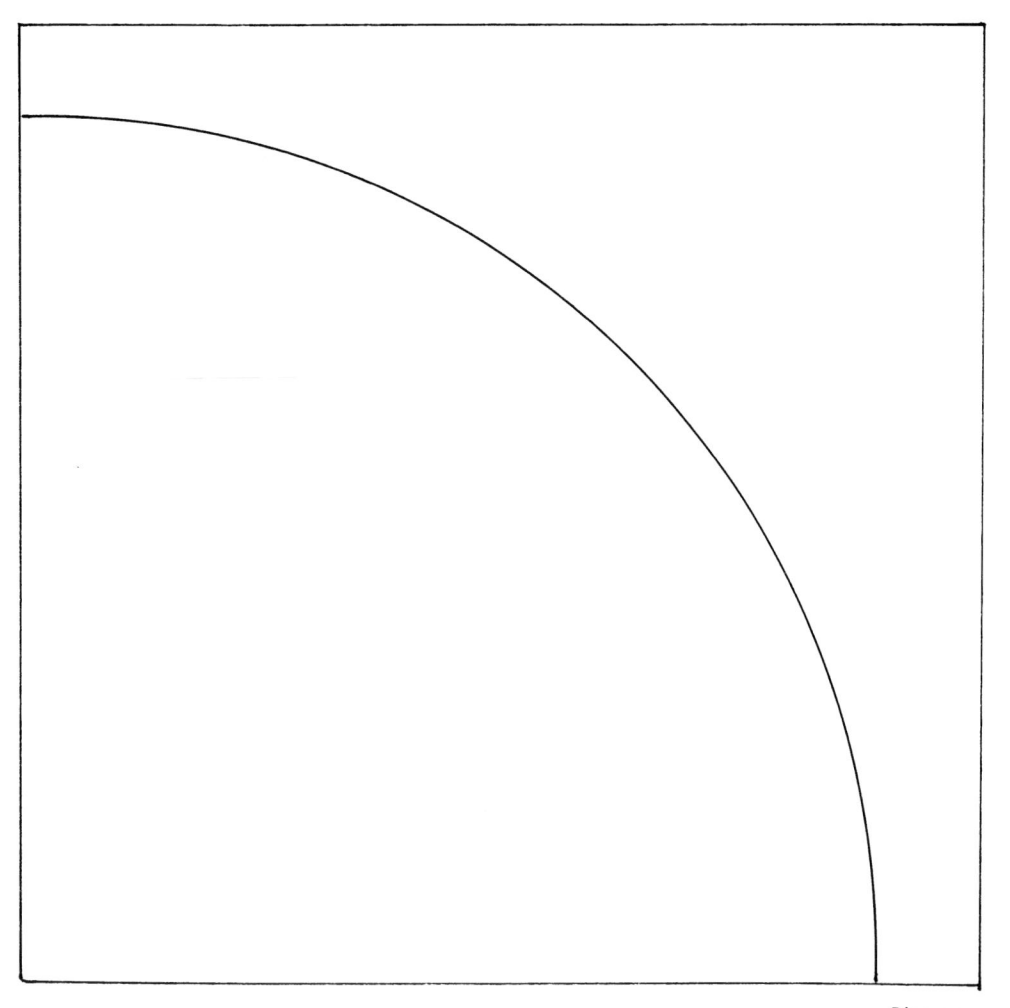

Diagram 1

template. Place the template in the middle of the card, use a pencil to draw the shapes that you wish to cut out and prick the holes. Place the template next to the holes and repeat the procedure. Do the embroidery before cutting out the shapes. Cut out the picture and stick it on the card. Cut out the separate parts according to the pattern, shape them and stick them on the background picture. Colour the border stickers and stick them between the embroidery.

3. Cat on a square card with a circle
What you need
- ❏ Card: brilliant silver (P162) and metallic (P143)
- ❏ Sticker sheet: silver borders
- ❏ Hobby pen: green
- ❏ Embossing template: EF18024
- ❏ Sulky thread: metallic mint
- ❏ Adhesive stones
- ❏ Fairyland cutting sheet: Cat (GW01)

Make a card which measures 13 x 26 cm. Cut the front of the card diagonally through the middle with a semicircle along the line of the cut. Place the template on the front of the card and use adhesive tape to stick it in place. Copy the shapes which you wish to cut out and prick the holes. Remove the template from the card. Do the embroidery before cutting out the shapes. Once you have cut out the shapes, stick the green card behind the openings. Cut out the picture and stick it on the card. Cut out the separate parts according to the cutting pattern, shape them and use 3D glue to stick them on the background picture. Colour the border sticker and stick it on the card.

4. Cat with half stars in the corners
What you need
- ❏ Card: brilliant silver (P162) and metallic card (P143)
- ❏ Sticker sheet: silver borders
- ❏ Hobby pen: green
- ❏ Embossing template: EF18024
- ❏ Sulky thread: metallic mint
- ❏ Adhesive stones
- ❏ Fairyland cutting sheet: Cat (GW01)

Make a card which measures 15 x 21 cm. Place the template in the corner and stick it in place. Use a pencil to draw the shapes that you wish to cut out and prick the holes. Do the same in all four corners. Do the embroidery before cutting out the shapes. Stick green card behind the openings. Cut out the picture and stick it on the card. Cut out the separate parts according to the cutting pattern, shape them and stick them on the background picture. Colour the border sticker and stick it between the embroidery.

1.

2.

3.

4.

FAIRYLAND 9

Dancing elves

1. Mermaid with an embroidered square
What you need:
- Card: Perla light blue (P139)
- Embossing template: EH1812
- Super stencil: SU4001
- Sulky thread: multi silver/copper/blue
- Fairyland cutting sheet: Elves in a river (GW06)

Make a card which measures 13 x 26 cm. Place the embossing template on a light box, place the card on top and copy the pattern. Cut out the shapes. Place the super stencil on the card and prick the border. Cut out the square and embroider the border. Cut out the picture and stick it inside the card. Cut out the mermaid on the rocks from another picture and stick it on the front of the card. Cut out the separate parts according to the pattern, shape them and stick them on the mermaid.

2. Elves dancing in a circle
What you need
- Card: brilliant pink (P164)
- Ready-made card: metallic copper (H81-54)
- Sulky thread: metallic light copper
- Embossing template: EF8009
- Fairyland cutting sheet: Dancing elves (GW03)

Make a card which measures 15 x 21 cm. Cut a pink card (9.5 x 14 cm). Place the template on the front of the card, decide where you wish to have the pattern and stick it in place. Prick the holes in the card. Turn the card over, place it on a light box and use an embossing stylus to copy the pattern. Embroider the card and stick it on the other card. Cut out the picture and stick it on the card. Cut out the separate parts, shape them and stick them on the background picture.

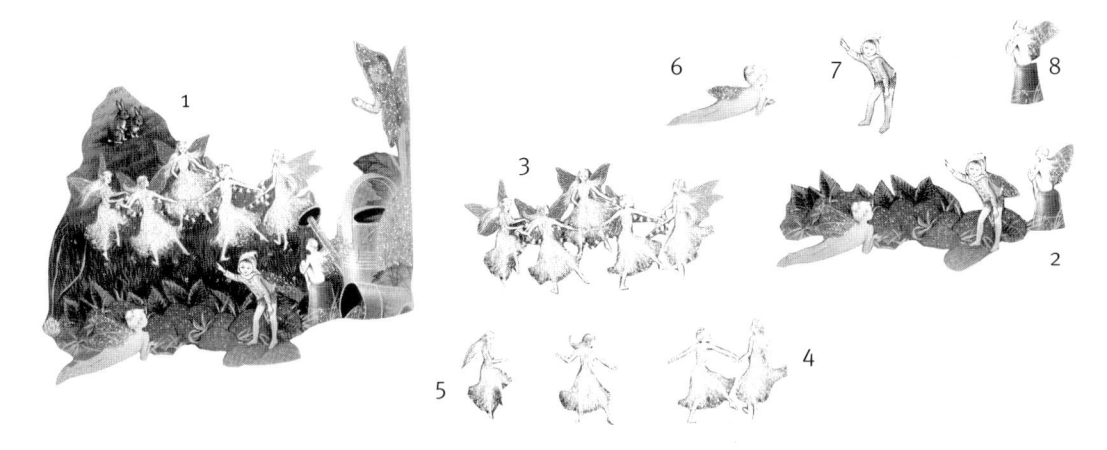

3. Elves in an oval

What you need
- Card: brilliant pink (P164)
- Ready-made card: metallic copper (H81-54)
- Fiskars cutting template: oval
- Border punch: bow
- Fairyland cutting sheet: Dancing elves (GW03)

Cut an oval in the pink card and punch the bows in the sides of the card. Cut out the picture and stick it behind the oval opening. Cut out the elves and stick them on the front of the card. Cut out the other pieces, shape them and stick them on the background picture.

4. Painting

What you need
- Card: metallic sapphire blue (H81-35), metallic bronze (H81-50) and brilliant pink (P164)
- Sticker sheets: gold corner ornaments and white borders
- Fairyland cutting sheet: Elves in a river (GW06)
- Foam tape

Cut a blue square (14.5 x 14.5 cm), a bronze square (13 x 13 cm) and a pink square (12 x 12 cm) with an aperture. Cut the picture out and stick it behind the pink card. Cut the separate pieces out according to the cutting pattern, shape them and stick them on the background picture. Allow everything to dry. Stick a couple of pieces of foam tape on the back of the bronze square and stick it to the blue square. Stick stickers in the corners and stick border stickers around the painting.

1.

2.

3.

4.

| 12 | **DANCING ELVES**

1.
2.
3.
4.

ELVES ON A TREE-STUMP 13

Elves on a tree-stump

1. Triangle with an elf
What you need:
- Card: brilliant pink (P164) and metallic green (P143)
- Embossing template: EF8009
- Sticker sheet: silver butterflies and borders
- Sulky thread: purple
- Hobby pen: purple
- Fairyland cutting sheet: Elf on a tree-stump (GW37)

Make a card which measures 15 x 21 cm. Cut a pink card (10.5 x 15 cm). Place the template on a light box, place the pink card on top and use an embossing stylus to copy the pattern as shown in the photograph. Prick the holes in the card. Embroider the card. Cut the front of the green card diagonally through the middle and stick the pink card inside. Cut out the picture and stick it on the front of the card. Cut out the separate parts, shape them and stick them on the background picture. Use the hobby pen to colour the border sticker and stick it along the diagonal cut on the front of the card. Use a drop of glue to stick the butterfly on the pink paper and colour it in.

2. Elf with butterflies
What you need
- Card: brilliant pink (P164) and metallic green (P143)
- Sticker sheet: silver butterflies
- Hobby pen: purple
- Picturel vellum: spring flowers
- Fairyland cutting sheet: Elf on a tree-stump (GW37)

Make a card which measures 13 x 26 cm. Cut a rectangle (9 x 12 cm). Stick the vellum on the card and stick the green card on the vellum. Cut out the picture and stick it on the card. Cut out the separate parts, shape them and stick them on the background picture. Stick the butterflies on the pink card. Use the hobby pen to colour them in and use a small amount of silicon glue to stick them on the card.

3. Elf on a square card with flowers
What you need
- Card: brilliant pink (P164) and metallic green (P143)
- Picturel vellum: spring flowers
- Feather

14 ELVES ON A TREE-STUMP

- Stickles
- Fairyland cutting sheet:
  Elf on a tree-stump (GW37)

Make a card which measures 13 x 26 cm. Cut a green square (10 x 10 cm). Stick the green card on the card and stick the feather on it. Cut the picture out and stick it on the feather. Cut out the separate parts, shape them and stick them on the background picture. Cut the flowers out of the vellum and use drops of silicon glue to stick them on the card. Add some glitter to the feather.

4. Circle with an elf

What you need
- Card: brilliant pink (P164) and metallic green (P143)
- Sticker sheet: silver borders
- Embossing stencil: round frame
- Adhesive stones
- Hobby pen: purple
- Fairyland cutting sheet:
  Elf on a tree-stump (GW37)

Make a card which measures 15 x 21 cm. Use the circle cutter to cut a circle (Ø 10 cm). Place the template on a light box, place the circle on top and use an embossing stylus to copy the shapes. Stick the circle on the card. Use the hobby pen to colour a border sticker purple and stick it on the circle. Cut out the picture and stick it partly on the circle. Cut out the other parts according to the cutting pattern, shape them and stick them on the background picture. Stick adhesive stones on the circle.

ELVES ON A TREE-STUMP 15

In love

1. Embroidered square card

What you need
- ❏ Card: Perla light blue (P139) and pearl paper
- ❏ Ornare pricking template: PR0501
- ❏ Sulky thread: metallic peacock blue
- ❏ Fairyland cutting sheet: Castle with a prince and princess (GW02)

Make a card which measures 13 x 26 cm.
Cut two squares (12 x 12 cm and 11.5 x 11.5 cm.

If you want to embroider the card, place the pricking template on the card and then prick and embroider the pattern. Stick the squares on the card. Cut out the picture and stick it partly

1.

2.

3.

IN LOVE 17

on the embroidered pattern. Cut out all the separate parts, shape them and stick them on the background picture.

2. Square card with a mirror

What you need
- ❏ Card: Perla light blue (P139) and pearl paper
- ❏ Mirror
- ❏ Adhesive stones
- ❏ Paper shapers: CSL05C and CSH05C (H)
- ❏ Fairyland cutting sheet: Castle with a prince and princess (GW02)

Make a card which measures 13 x 26 cm. Cut a square (8 x 8 cm) using the pearl paper. Cut three squares (5 x 5 cm). Use one punch to punch a corner and then use the other punch to punch in the same corner over the other punched pattern, i.e. use two punches in each corner. Stick the square on the card and stick the mirror on top. Stick the punched squares against the edge. Cut the picture out and stick it on the mirror. Cut out the other parts, shape them and stick them on the background picture. Decorate the card with adhesive stones.

3. In love

What you need
- ❏ Card: Perla yellow (P141), Perla light blue (P139) and metallic gold-white (H81-05)
- ❏ Sticker sheet: white borders
- ❏ Embossing template: EH1810
- ❏ Fairyland cutting sheet: Castle with a prince and princess (GW02)

Make a card which measures 13 x 26 cm. Cut two squares (12.5 x 12.5 cm and 11.5 x 11.5 cm). Place the template on a light box and place the square (11.5 x 11.5 cm) on top. Copy the pattern in the corners and cut out the small pieces. Stick everything on the card. Cut out the picture and stick it on the card. Cut out the separate parts, shape them and stick them on the background picture. Stick the border sticker around the card.

18 IN LOVE

Elf on a toadstool

1. Square embroidered card

What you need:
- ❏ Card: metallic green (P143)
- ❏ Ready-made card: metallic gold white (H81-04)
- ❏ Embossing template: EF8009
- ❏ Sulky thread: Christmas green
- ❏ Fairyland cutting sheet: Elf story (GW35)

Place the template on a light box. Place the card on top of the template and copy the pattern. Prick the holes and embroider the card. Cut a rectangle (10 x 12.5 cm) out of green card. Cut out the picture and stick it on the card. Cut out the separate parts, shape them and stick them on the background picture.

2. Embroidered oval

What you need
- ❏ Card: Perla light green (P138) and metallic gold white (H81-05)
- ❏ Sulky thread: Christmas green
- ❏ Embossing template: EF8022
- ❏ Fairyland cutting sheet: Elf story (GW35)

Make a card which measures 15 x 21 cm. Place the template on a light box and copy part of the pattern in the corners. Prick the holes and embroider them. Cut the small pieces out and stick light green card behind the openings. Cut out the picture and stick it inside the card. Cut out the separate parts according to the cutting pattern, shape them and stick them on the background picture.

3. Embossed oval

What you need
- ❏ Card: Perla light green (P138) and metallic gold white (H81-05)
- ❏ Sticker sheet: silver borders
- ❏ Hobby pen: green
- ❏ Adhesive stones
- ❏ Fairyland cutting sheet: Elf story (GW35)
- ❏ Embossing template: EF8009

Make a card which measures 15 x 21 cm. Place the template on a light box, place the card on top and copy the pattern in the corners. Stick the light green card behind the oval and cut it to the correct size. Use the hobby pen to colour the border sticker and stick it around the oval. Cut out the picture and stick it on the card. Cut out the other parts according to the pattern, shape them and stick them on the background picture. Use Tacky glue to stick adhesive stones on the card. Stick sticker dots in the oval.

4. Square card

What you need
- Card: Perla light green (P138) and metallic (P143)
- Ready-made card: metallic gold-white (H81-04)
- Sticker sheet: silver borders
- Adhesive stones
- Fairyland cutting sheet: Elf story (GW35)
- Embossing template: EH1813
- Hobby pen: green
- Figure punch: daisy

Place the template on a light box, place the pink card on top and copy the pattern in the corners. Cut out the shapes and stick light green card behind the openings. Place the template on the light green card and cut the shape out. Repeat this with the picture and stick it on the card. Cut out the separate parts according to the cutting pattern, shape them and stick them on the background picture. Use the green hobby pen to colour in the border sticker and stick it in the corners. Stick adhesive stones on the card. Punch the daisies, stick them in the corners and stick an adhesive stone on them.

20 ELF ON A TOADSTOOL

1.

2.

3.

4.

ELF ON A TOADSTOOL | 21

Swan elf

1. Round card

What you need
- Card: brilliant pink (P164)
- Embossing template: flower frame
- Adhesive stones
- Fairyland cutting sheet: Swan journey (GW34)

Make a card which measures 13 x 26 cm. Place the template on the card, use adhesive tape to stick it in place and use a pencil to draw around the circumference. Turn the card over, place it on a light box and copy the pattern. Cut along the line that you have drawn. Do not cut one of the sides. Cut out all the small pieces. Cut out the picture and make it 3D. Decorate the card with adhesive stones and sticker dots.

2. Card with a window

What you need
- Card: brilliant pink (P164)
- Mica
- Sticker sheet: silver ornament
- Stickles: blue and pink
- Fairyland cutting sheet: Swan journey (GW34)
- Embossing template: flower frame

Make a card which measures 13 x 26 cm. Place the template on the card where you wish to have the pattern and use a pencil to copy the template (this will be cut out later). Turn the card over, place it on a light box and copy the pattern. Cut out the middle piece. Stick the sticker on the mica and then stick it behind the opening. Use the Stickles to colour it in and allow it to dry. Cut out the picture and make it 3D. Stick sticker dots on the card.

3. Card with two windows

What you need
- Card: brilliant pink (P164)
- Sticker sheets: silver ornament and holographic borders
- Mica
- Stickles: pink and blue
- Fairyland cutting sheet: Swan journey (GW34)
- Embossing template: flower frame

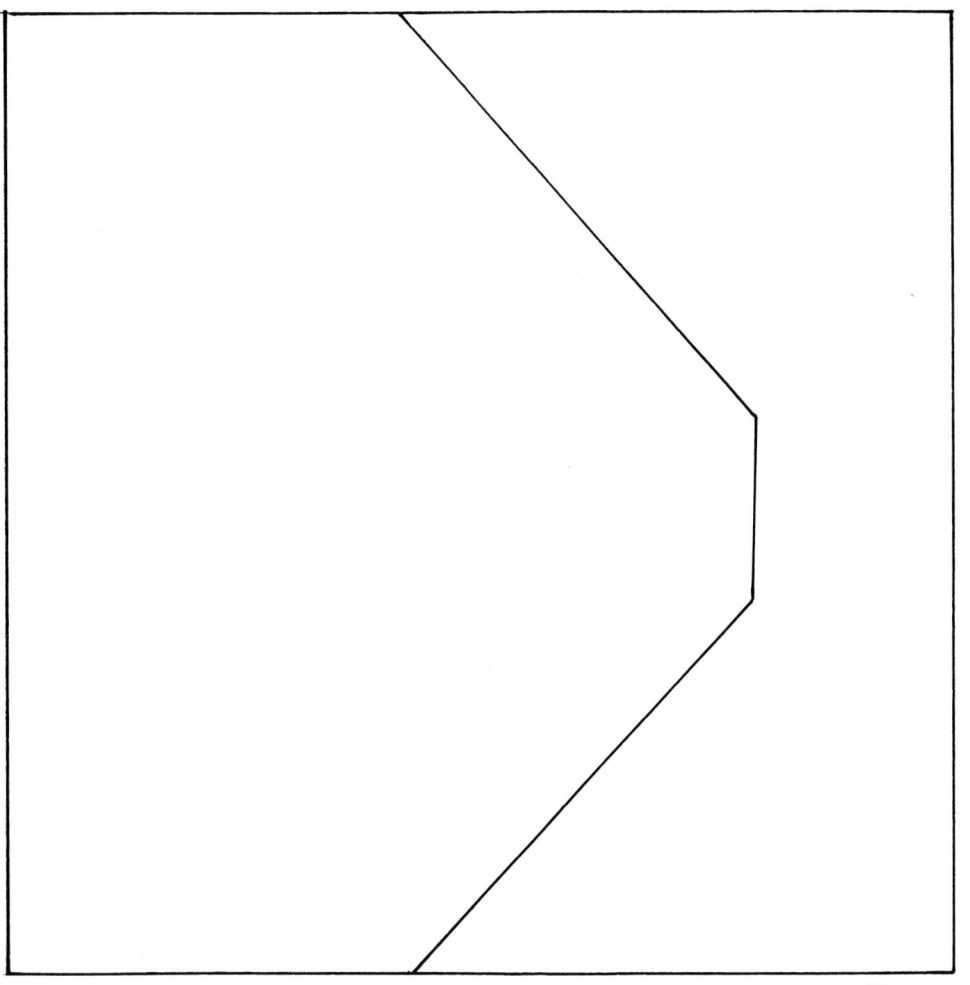

Diagram 2

Make a card which measures 13 x 26 cm. Cut out the picture with two sloping sides (see diagram 2) and stick it on the card. Place the template on the card and copy what you wish to cut. Turn the card over, place it on a light box and copy the pattern. Stick the sticker on the mica and use Stickles to colour it in. Allow it to dry. Stick the mica behind the openings. Stick the border sticker along the edge of the picture. Cut out the picture and make it 3D.

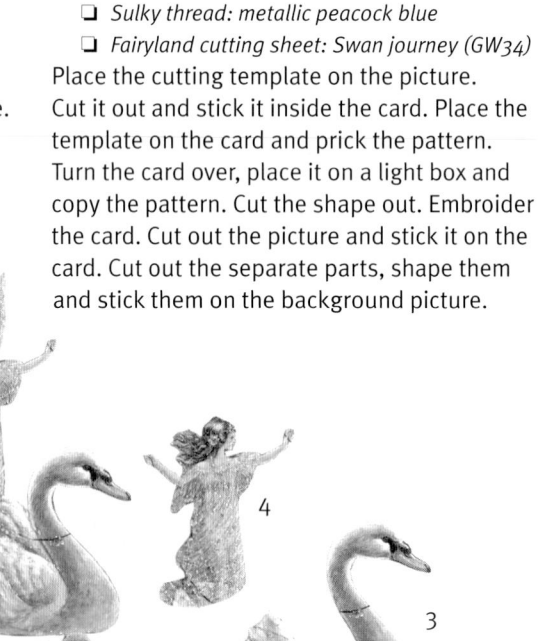

4. Embroidered card with an elf
What you need
- *Zigzag card*
- *Fiskars cutting template: frames*
- *Embossing template EF8002*
- *Sulky thread: metallic peacock blue*
- *Fairyland cutting sheet: Swan journey (GW34)*

Place the cutting template on the picture. Cut it out and stick it inside the card. Place the template on the card and prick the pattern. Turn the card over, place it on a light box and copy the pattern. Cut the shape out. Embroider the card. Cut out the picture and stick it on the card. Cut out the separate parts, shape them and stick them on the background picture.

SWAN ELF

1.

2.

3.

4.

SWAN ELF 25

Fairy-tale wedding

1. Square card with a punched rectangle
What you need
- Card: mother-of-pearl white (H81-00) and pearl paper
- Ornare pricking template: PR0501
- Paper shapers: CSH05C and CSL05C (H)
- Adhesive stones
- Fairyland cutting sheet:
  Fairy-tale wedding (GW36)

Make a card which measures 13 x 26 cm. Cut two rectangles (8 x 13 cm and 6.5 x 12 cm). Place the template on the card and prick the pattern in the corners. Embroider the pattern. Use the first punch to punch the corners and then use the second punch to punch over the top of the first punch. These two punches fit over each other. Slide the white card through the punched patterns. Stick everything on the card. Cut out the picture and stick it on the card. Cut out the separate parts, shape them and stick them on the background picture. Decorate the card with adhesive stones.

2. Embroidered card with a mirror
What you need
- Card: mother-of-pearl white (H81-00) and pearl paper
- Embossing template: EF8022
- Sulky thread: metallic peacock blue
- Mirror
- Adhesive stones
- Fairyland cutting sheet:
  Fairy-tale wedding (GW36)
- Figure scissors

Take a standard card. Place the template on the card and prick the pattern. Turn the card and the template over, place them on a light box and copy the pattern. Cut all the shapes out and embroider them. Make a circle (Ø 10 cm) and use the figure scissors to cut around the edge. Place the mirror on top of this. Cut the picture out and stick it on the mirror. Cut out the separate parts, shape them and stick them on the background picture. Decorate the card with adhesive stones.

3. Fairy-tale wedding

What you need
- ❏ Card: mother-of-pearl white (H81-00) and pearl paper
- ❏ Embossing template: EH1812
- ❏ Fairyland cutting sheet: Fairy-tale wedding (GW36)

Make a card which measures 13 x 26 cm. Place the template on a light box and place the card on top. Copy the pattern and cut out the shapes. Cut out the picture and stick it on the card. Cut out the separate parts, shape them and stick them on the background picture.

FAIRY-TALE WEDDING 27

1.

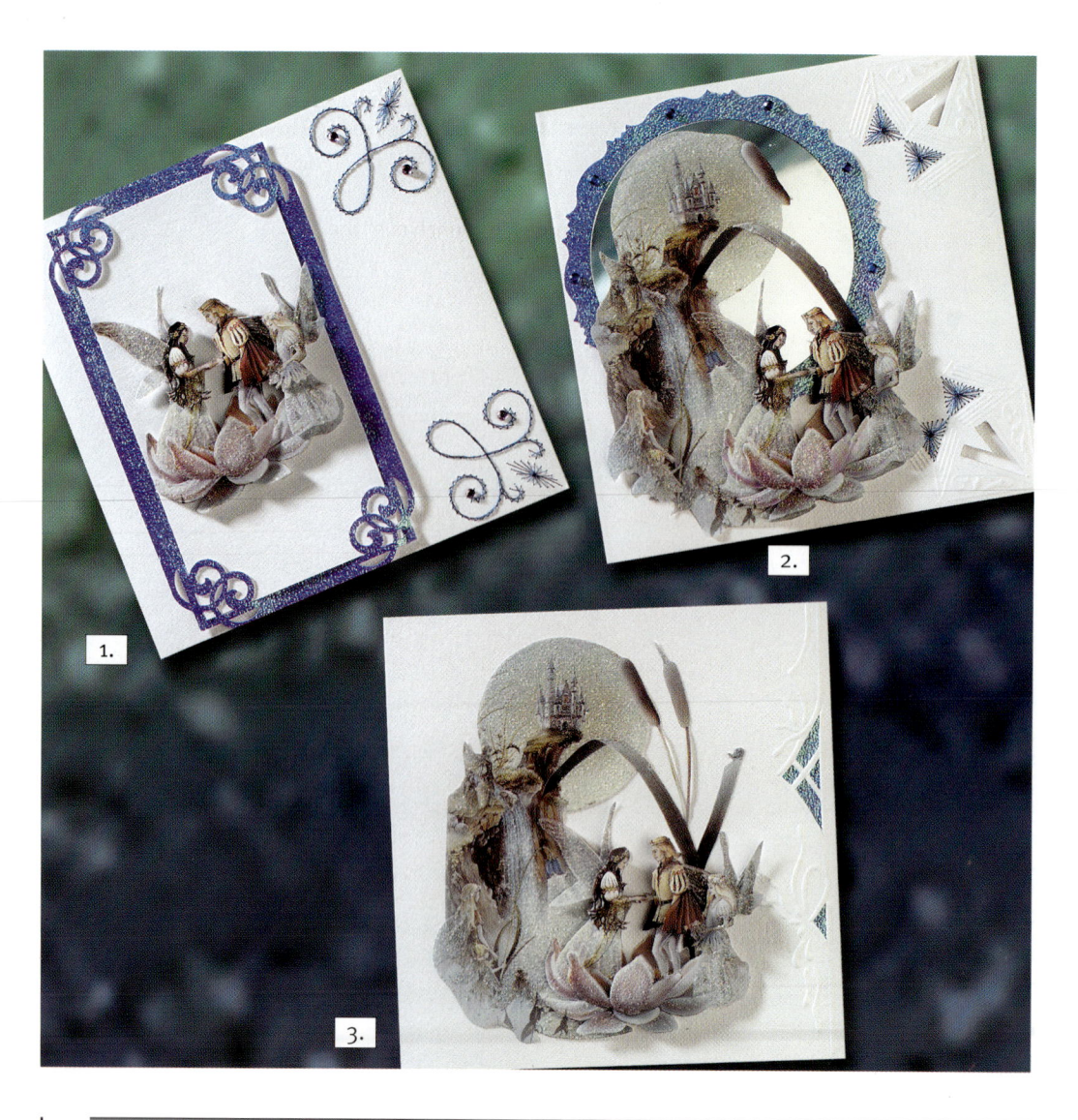

2.

3.

28 FAIRY-TALE WEDDING

CHRISTMAS IN FAIRYLAND 29

Christmas in Fairyland

1. Elves with a full moon

What you need
- Card: metallic sapphire blue (H81-35) and pearl paper
- Sticker sheet: silver ice crystal
- Adhesive stones
- Fairyland cutting sheet: Elves on a branch (GW05)
- Nel van Veen step-by-step sheet: 2234
- Embossing templates: EH1812 and EH1810

Make a card which measures 13 x 26 cm. Cut a square (13 x 13 cm) out of the pearl paper. Cut a square (9 x 9 cm) out of the bottom right-hand corner. Place the pearl paper and the templates on a light box and copy the patterns. Cut the shapes out and stick it on the card. Cut out the picture and stick it on the card. Cut out the separate parts, shape them and stick them on the background picture. Stick the border sticker between the embossed areas. Stick adhesive stones on the stickers. Stick a poinsettia in the corner.

2. Princess with a mirror

What you need
- Card: metallic sapphire blue (H81-35) and metallic pearl white (H81-00)
- Mirror
- Figure scissors
- Sticker sheet: silver ice crystal
- Embossing templates: EH1812, EH1810 and oval frame
- Adhesive stones
- Fairyland cutting sheet: Princess on the moon (GW04)
- Nel van Veen step-by-step sheet: 2234

Make a card which measures 13 x 26 cm. Cut the front of the card diagonally in two. Cut a circle (Ø 10 cm) out of white card. Place the round template on a light box, place the circle on top and copy the pattern. Stick the circle on the card so that it protrudes over the edge of the cut. Copy the pattern and use the figure scissors to cut around the edge of the circle. Place the template on a light box, place the white card on top and copy the pattern in the corners and along the sides. Cut the shapes out

and stick it inside the card. Place the mirror on the front of the circle, being careful not to leave any fingerprints. Cut the picture out and stick it on the mirror. Cut out the separate parts, shape them and stick them on the background picture. Stick the border sticker around the edge.
Cut out the flowers and stick them on the card. Decorate the card with adhesive stones.

3. Princess on the moon

What you need
- ❏ Card: metallic sapphire blue (H81-35) and metallic pearl white (H81-00)
- ❏ Figure scissors
- ❏ Sticker sheet: silver ice crystal
- ❏ Adhesive stones
- ❏ Fairyland cutting sheet: Princess on the moon (GW04)
- ❏ Nel van Veen step-by-step sheet: 2234

Make a card which measures 13 x 26 cm. Cut four strips out of the white card and stick them on the card. Cut a square (9.5 x 9.5 cm), use the figure scissors to cut along the edges and stick it on the card. Cut out the picture and stick it on the card. Cut out the separate parts, shape them and stick them on the background picture. Stick the border sticker on the strips and stick adhesive stones on them. Cut out some holly leaves and stick them on the card.

4. Elves on a branch

What you need
- ❏ Card: metallic sapphire blue (H81-35) and metallic pearl white (H81-00)
- ❏ Figure scissors
- ❏ Sticker sheet: silver ice crystal
- ❏ Fairyland cutting sheet: Elves on a branch (GW05)
- ❏ Nel van Veen step-by-step sheet: 2234
- ❏ Adhesive stones
- ❏ Embossing template EH1810

Cut a card (13 x 26 cm) according to diagram 3. Cut a square (8.5 x 8.5 cm) and use the figure scissors to cut around the edges. Cut three triangles and use the figure scissors to cut along one side. Place the template on a light box with the triangles on top and copy the pattern. Cut the shapes out. Cut two strips, cut along both sides with the figure scissors and stick them on the card. Stick the square on the card. Cut the picture out and stick it in the middle. Cut out the separate parts, shape them and stick them on the background picture. Make the birdhouse 3D. Stick a border sticker on the strips and stick adhesive stones on top.

Diagram 3:
Increase in size by 125%

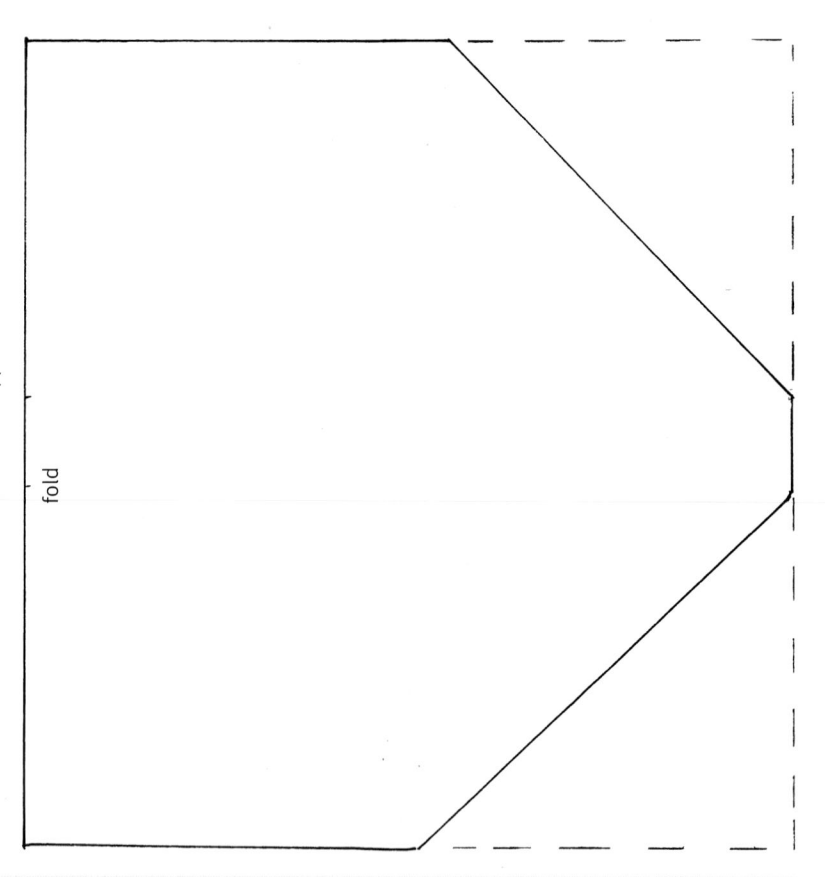

Many thanks to Papicolor International B.V. in Utrecht, the Netherlands, Avec B.V. in Waalwijk, the Netherlands, Kars en Co B.V. in Ochten, the Netherlands, Mariëtte Verhees in 's-Hertogenbosch, the Netherlands, Else Plantinga Design and De Hobbyzolder in Venhuizen, the Netherlands for providing the materials.

See www.creatief.info for information on where to purchase Fairyland cutting sheets. If you are not able to buy them, contact De Hobbyzolder in Venhuizen, the Netherlands (+31 (0)228 544244) or see www.dehobbyzolder.nl for more information. There is a fan club for Else at www.clubs.nl.